THE LAWYER'S OATH.

AN ADDRESS

DELIVERED BEFORE THE

CLASS OF 1867,

OF THE

LAW DEPARTMENT,

UNIVERSITY OF MICHIGAN,

MARCH 27th, 1867,

By D. BETHUNE DUFFIELD, Esq.

ANN ARBOR:
DR. CHASE'S STEAM PRINTING HOUSE.
1867.

At a meeting of the members of the Law Department, University of Michigan, March 27th, 1867, the following resolution was adopted:

Resolved, That our sincere thanks are due to D. BETHUNE DUFFIELD, Esq., for his able and interesting Address before the Graduating Class of the Law Department, at the Eighth Annual Commencement, and that we respectfully solicit a copy for publication.

ADDRESS.

Mr. President, Honorable Professors, and Gentlemen:

Hitherto, on these occasions, you have had Judges of distinguished ability speaking to you from their high places, words of choice wisdom and high incentive.

To-day it is appointed you to hear the more humble and hurried words of one coming directly from the busy Bar; and who, while bidding you welcome to that toiling circle, offers for your consideration such suggestions as seem appropriate to those who, without the experience of professional life, have yet to grapple with its difficulties, yet to en counter its temptations, yet to carve their way and leave their record along its crowded avenues.

Law, in the most comprehensive acceptation of the term, implies the enactment of all those principles of Virtue which are binding on mankind, as members of Society. Its ministers, therefore, should be pre-eminently men of virtue. All civilized communities, as a means of testing the moral fitness of the man for this high service, as well as of securing his allegiance to the State, have, consequently, prescribed and exacted from those who would assume the responsibility of expounding and executing these principles, a solemn oath.

In no Country, perhaps, where the same degree of liberty prevailed among the people, did the code of laws touch so many interests of public, family, and individual life, as in the old city of Geneva; which as a Free Republic, defiantly braved the storm of centuries in the very heart of Monarchical Europe; and by no community were the laws more rigorously enforced or faithfully observed. Indeed, it may be said of them that "in this sign,"—loyalty to law,—was their conquest both achieved and maintained.

Hearken, then, to the Genevan Advocate's oath, as it has come down to us from this vigorous people, and remember that though its *ipsissima verba* may not be found in the simpler form of oath you take on the morrow, still its stern and pure precepts are written all over the lofty frieze of that venerable temple into whose chambers you propose presently to pass.

"I solemnly swear before Almighty God to be faithful to the Repub-
"lic, and the Canton of Geneva; never to depart from the respect due

"to the tribunals and authorities; never to counsel or maintain a cause "which does not appear to be just or equitable, unless it be the defense "of an accused person; never to employ, knowingly, for the purpose of "maintaining the causes confided to me, any means contrary to truth; "and never to seek to mislead the Judges by any artifice or false state- "ment of fact or law; to abstain from all offensive personality, and to "advance no fact contrary to the honor or reputation of the parties, if it "be not indispensable to the cause with which I may be charged; not to "encourage either the commencement or continuance of a suit from any "motive of passion or interest; not to reject for any consideration per- "sonal to myself, the cause of the weak, the stranger, or the oppressed."

My young friends, here you have the creed of the upright and honorable lawyer. The clear, stern, and lofty language in which it is expressed, needs no argument to elucidate its principles, no eloquence to enforce its obligations. It has in it the sacred savor of Divine inspiration, and sounds almost like a restored reading from Sinai's original, but broken tablets.

The general subject I propose, therefore, to consider with you on this occasion is *The Lawyer's Oath, its Obligations, and some of the Duties springing out of them.*

And first, the Oath, by its very terms, assumes that every Lawyer is, or should properly be, a man of positive virtue. For he counsels his neighbor as to his rights and duties in all the varying experiences of human life, commercial, social, domestic, personal. And that we may correctly understand what is meant by rights and duties, it may be well here to define them. Rights, exactly considered, may be designated as the free enjoyment of such privileges as are conceded to men under the Divine laws, and such human laws as are in harmony therewith; while Duties may be set forth as the fulfillment of our obligations under the same laws, both to God and our fellow men. It is in the light of duty thus defined, that the Lawyer receives from the faltering lips of some dying client, the whispers of direction for the disposition of his entire estate; and yields his last earthly autograph to the paper which his Counsel tells him contains all those directions appropriately expressed. It is in a just appreciation of these rights and duties, that the Counsellor and Advocate stands between the scaffold or the prison door on the one hand, and the crouching, trembling prisoner on the other, who with "strong crying and tears," perhaps, commits both liberty and life into his keeping. The sacredness and magnitude of these interests then, as well as the grave responsibilities growing out of them, all presuppose and imperatively demand the very highest traits of character in the attorney and counselor at law. Every high-minded and cultivated community, too, will demand a high-minded and cultivated Bar; regarding it as the very surest bulwark of defense to their liberties. And where such a Bar has been displaced by one corrupt and unscrupulous, it will be sure to be found among a corrupt and demoralized people, where virtue, liberty, and good morals have all gone down together.

Moreover, it is from the Bar that the Bench is made. He who, to-day, pleads the cause of his client, may, in the next year sit as a judge over the same citizen; and in the same degree that he shared the confidence of that Client, while he served him as counsel, will he enjoy his confidence while passing upon his controversies as Judge.

This elevating thought should of itself inspire and strengthen every Lawyer to walk uprightly and to maintain his integrity as spotlessly as if the ermine was already upon his robe and the signet-seal of authority in his hand. For a reckless, unprincipled practitioner at the Bar, if he shall once attain to the Bench, will find many of his professional acts returning suddenly as plagues upon his peace; and they will then plant thorns not only in the purple velvets of his official chair, but far down in the tender depths of an ever wakeful and troubled conscience.

Viewed aright, there is a truly grand distinction for him who is called to fill the great Executive department of this nation of Nations. There is honor also in the Legislative branch of the Government, stretching its controlling arm of power from the Lakes to the Gulf, from the Atlantic to the Pacific coasts; but in the Judiciary, where really are lodged the liberty of the citizen, the security of the people, the real life of the Nation, there are honors which cannot be outweighed by any that either Crown or Sceptre confers. We cannot too highly respect, honor, and defend this stronghold of liberty, this God-given altar of peace among us; for here, *necessarily*, under our system, must be the limit of controversy, the end of strife.

History informs us, that this office has ever commanded the respect and obedience of every cultivated people; and if we stretch our observations as far back as Moses and the Theocracy, we shall find that the Judge was the highest officer of power, in that form of government, combining the Executive with the Judiciary function. Above and higher than him there was but one, and He was God. "Judge righteously," says Moses, "between every man and his brother, and the stranger that "is with thee, for the judgment is God's."--Deut. I, 16 and 17. And Jehosa phat, when addressing the Judges whom he had appointed over the land, after the Theocracy had given place to the Monarchy, still says: "Take heed what ye do, for ye judge not for man, but for the Lord who "is with you in the judgment; for there is no iniquity with the Lord our "God, nor respect of persons, nor taking of gifts."—2d Chron., chapter XIX, ver. 6 and 7. At this late day it will hardly be denied by those who enjoy a Christian civilization, that all lawful dominion, in the abstract, is of God; and that he has ordained and, in his providence, does still ordain governments among men, to protect and secure the rights of man, "life, liberty, and the pursuit of happiness." He also ordains the means necessary and fit to attain those ends. True, He has not or does not designate these means in detail; He could not do so; for they would necessarily vary in different ages, climates, and states of society, He has decided that human life shall be secure, the rights of property guarded, and civil society protected, but leaves the particular theories or forms of government necessary to secure all these ends to man's own choice. He refers them, however, for great principles, to His own code, which, in its broad extent, furnishes to-day, the ground-work of a large portion of our several State Statute laws. Nevertheless, from the fact that He has instituted this high office of Judge, and set it in all its purity above all other authority, not excepting the King himself, we are to understand that it still exists in the world as of Divine appointment, and demands the supreme obedience of the people. Therefore it is that the first obligation imposed by the oath we have read in your hearing, after the pledge of allegiance to the Republic, is, "never to depart from the "respect due to the tribunals and authorities."

In this Country, where we make our liberty too much a matter of boastful pride, there has of late years grown up a sort of tendency, (not always confined to the ruder classes of the people,) to depreciate, often to put open disrespect upon the Magistracy—so far as it may be done safely. The motive which prompts this unhappy exhibition of indignity, if analyzed, would, perhaps, in the majority of instances, be found to spring out of a boorish pride in what is supposed to be the liberty of the American citizen. Still it has its mischievous influence in society, gradually diminishing the authority, as it detracts from the dignity of these tribunals, and ought to be checked and rebuked wherever an opportunity so to do occurs. Certainly such barbaric license should never be tolerated, much less attempted by those whose life is spent in the presence of the Judges. Indeed it is not inappropriate here to remark, that Courts of Justice in this Country, from the fact that they have dispensed perhaps with quite too much of the old ceremonials designed to command the popular respect, stand now in special need of all the assistance the Bar can render them, in upholding before the masses the power and majesty of the Law. Evil consequences in various forms are already showing themselves in society, growing out of this unhappy tendency among us; and it behooves every Lawyer in the land to set himself as a barrier against its further extension. No better mode of counteracting this mischief can be suggested than for the Lawyer, by his own example, to show before others, that respect which he concedes to be due from him to the occupants of the Bench. Nor will he in so doing feel that he is in any wise demeaning himself. Sir Thomas More, whose head fell on Tower Hill because he would not prostitute the law to Royal requirement, while Lord High Chancellor of England, did not hesitate to kneel down, as he passed the door of an inferior court in Westminister Hall, and solicit, on bended knee, the blessing of his father, who sat as a Judge in that Court. It is not so much the man that is seen in that dread place of power, as it is the Divinely appointed minister of Justice, the upholder of law, the protector of life, liberty and property, the defender of religion, and the avenger of crime.

In the further general consideration of this subject of professional in tegrity, we may be allowed to refer to one or two false notions somewhat current with respect to the duty of Lawyers, and not always entertained by those outside the profession. They may appropriately be considered in connection with the third clause of the oath,—" never to counsel or " maintain a cause which does not appear to be just or equitable ; unless " it be the defense of an accused person." Under this clause, may a Lawyer properly advocate a bad cause ? There are some Lawyers who will tell you that he may ; affirming that a Lawyer is not at liberty to refuse his services to *any* person, and that once engaged, he is bound to employ every means in his power to win success to his client. In support of this cold-steel style of practice. they will refer you to so eminent a person as Lord Brougham, who, in the British House of Lords, is reported to have said that, " the advocate is bound to forget that there is any other person in the world but his client, and to lose sight of every other consideration than that of success." But can this be really so? Has the Lawyer sold himself body, brains, and soul to his client for a ten or a twenty dollar fee ? Has he not obligations resting upon him superior to those of the contract of client and attorney ? Does he not owe duties to society at large, to good morals, to his own conscience, and the God to whom that concience makes report ? Must he, for example, put off not only all morality, but all tenderness of heart and all self-respect, and surrender his talents and his conscience, to the first notorious gambler or courtezan that would fain rob successfully the unwary youth, or persecute and destroy fallen innocence ? Must he hire himself out to the usurious money-lender, who would take from the widow and her children, the last bed and blanket, and turn them, as his " legal right," into the dreary darkness of a winter's night ? God forbid !

But the man who advocates the affirmative of this proposition, must go all lengths. He must answer these fearful interrogatories also in the affirmative. And generally, they who hold to tenets of this kind, are found capable of executing all such behests as these. They are of those who are cursed with a love of money, with whom it has become a passion. They will work for it, fight for it ; beg, lie, and die for it. Yea, they will sacrifice on the altar of this insatiate Moloch, all the finer attributes of their humanity ; make merchandise of all that is sacred of

2

human affections ; and to crown the high summit of their guilt, profanely announce before the very altar of Justice, that if these various enormities are only perpetrated under a legal writ, or some form or color of law, it is morally right ; because that which " the law admits, is always " right." I trust it is not necessary for you to be told, that when this principle is adopted by the legal profession, and approved by the Courts, it can only be, when the latter have long ceased to be tribunals for the administration of Justice, and Attorneys have become licensed robbers, and moral outlaws in society.

The Law, and all its machinery are means, not ends ; the purpose for which they are instituted is Justice, pure and simple ; not rapine and robbery; and the Lawyer who, in his zeal for the means, forgets the great ends of Law, betrays not only a corrupt heart but a feeble, or at least an unsound understanding. When a client then asks his Counsel for an opinion on any purely legal question, he is bound to answer, stating the law just as it is. But here his duty ends. If his client presses him to extend his counsel still farther, and direct him as to his future conduct, he must, as a moral and accountable being, point that client's feet into paths that lead to justice, not toward wrong and oppression. He, no more than any other man, can advise an immorality or an injustice ; and should he do so, and favor the unjust schemes of a bad client, he becomes equally guilty with him ; as much as if they two had originally conspired in malicious scheming against the peace or prosperity of their neighbor. Nor is the rule we here lay down, in conflict with the defense by Counsel, of a man whom he believes guilty. He may do this ; for the Law gives every accused person the benefit of a presumed innocence, until his guilt is duly established by the forms of law, and beyond a reasonable doubt, whatever his own surmises may be as to the guilt of his client. He cannot properly become his Judge, but is bound to lay before the jury, whatever circnmstances in the case operate to his client's advantage, or palliate the moral turpitude of the action, and so mitigate the degree of punishment. But when an evil minded man has perpetrated some bloody crime, and so outraged justice, and in the first throes of his passion or distress, freely and frankly confesses his guilt then he should pause well and long before assuming his defense. Professional pride, and a natural sympathy may incline him to the effort at release. A weeping wife and children exposed to orphanage and shame, may entreat him to rescue the father and the husband from the dread penalty of his offense ; but still the true and faithful Counselor will not forget his superior allegiance to the cause of Justice, nor his obligations to society at large ; and he will decide accordingly. Should his sympathies overcome his better judgment, and his own strong mind laboring at the Bar, before a weak or a too benevolent one upon the Bench, and sympathising natures in the jury box, succeed in acquitting the self-confessed criminal, and before another fortnight, that guilty client should add yet another murder to the one confessed, how think you would he view *his* responsibility in connection with this last offence? Would he not see, in such a case, that it would be better, far better, to act in loyalty to justice and the claims of society at large, rather than yield to the sympathetic promptings of an erring heart, and so release, and relicense the murderer to his "bloody business." The lawyer, therefore, should never lower the standard of his own integrity in doubtful cases; but always give to *Justice*, whose loyal servant he is, the benefit of the doubt. Thus will he best serve the cause of right and truth, while he secures the approval of that inflexible Judge within his own breast, before whose tribunal, specious arguments, and pleasing eloquence are all vain as the idle winds.

And now suffer a moment's reference to the fourth clause of the oath, "never to employ knowingly, for the purpose of maintaining the "causes confided to me, any means contrary to truth; and never to seek "to mislead the Judges by any artifice or false statement of fact or law." Conceding to every practitioner the average of integrity sufficient to carry him safely through the first half of this clause, it is on the last sentence that the real trial comes. For here, if anywhere, occurs the first and perhaps the most frequent deflections from the strict line of professional obligation. Looking back over an experience of now more than twenty years, I am free to confess that the natural dereliction of the lawyer, (if such an expression may be allowed) and by it I mean his failure to come up squarely to the front line and full measure of his duty before the Court, is *just here*. The Attorney becomes engaged, perhaps enthusiastically enlisted in the cause of his client, and gives himself to the work of trial-preparation with a zeal which blinds his eyes to any merits except such as appertain to his side of the case. Authorities and principles that militate against him, are sometimes artfully veiled, or wholly ignored in the argument. Consequently he overlooks or, at least, fails to appreciate the fact that this fervor of zeal, and partial advocacy may possibly mislead the judges, by a perversion or suppression of some feature of the case, which they *ought* to know and fully to understand. He does not, and apparently, cannot bring himself to a broad and generous presentation of both sides of the case, but rests contented with a preparation and submission of his own, leaving opposing Counsel to do as he has done. And if such Counsel, from inability, accident, or any other cause, should fail so to do, then he is quite willing to accept all advantages likely to accrue therefrom, should the Court chance to omit the assumption, and discharge this part of the labor in the case, for itself. This tendency is apt soon to take the form of habit, and to grow upon the Lawyer until ere long he begins to regard it as the natural form of procedure; and then it is a hard matter for him to do otherwise. And yet, before an intelligent and honest Judiciary, it is always better to be frank and open, generously to state the points of your adversary, as well as your own, combatting them the while, to the best of your ability, and so rendering to the Court an argument of the question which is truly valuable. The Court will thank you, and think more of you for this mode of discussing your case; for thus you help them forward to a just and fair conclusion. A very safe rule for the practitioner in this connection is, to so argue the case as you would wish to have it argued before yourself, if you were a Judge on the Bench. Suppress nothing, hide no case, conceal no material fact, cover up no legal principle, indulge in no illogical subtleties, but with a downright and honest loyalty to the Law first, and then to your client, deal openly, candidly, and honestly with the Court; and be assured you will never lose anything by it in the opinion of the court, even though their judgment be entered up against you. For in your case, at least, they will recognize the existence of what is popularly regarded as a myth, or at least a moral impossibility, viz., a good lawyer and an honest man in one and the same person!

But beyond the ordinary rules and amenities of practice, you should even regard it as your duty to be at all times, and under all circumstances, the friend, helper, and protector of the Court, not merely in respect to the individuality of its membership, but to the Court as a great and sacred institution for devising and distributing justice and security among the people. And estimating it at its true value as such, you will never suffer yourselves to be seduced by inexperience or designing men, contending blindly for what they see fit to call Law Reform, while, as a matter of fact, they often cover schemes of the most Utopian character, and which, if adopted, would seriously threaten not only the high conserving value of the Courts, as the people have hitherto enjoyed them, but even the entire and time-honored system of Jurisprudence on which they rest. True, there are not a few defects yet lurking in our legal and chancery practice, which we ought to remove or largely modify; but this is being done gradnally, and though they are slowly, they are still surely falling away from our laws and various codes of practise. But this reforming hand, like that which thrusts the pruning-knife among the branches of the vine, must ever move cautiously and with great discrimination, and occasionally it will even then lop off a branch which ought not to have been removed. For instance, it is a question of very grave doubt to-day, whether this reforming sentiment has not done an injury to our Courts of justice, as well as great moral injury to the community at large, by abolishing the old rule of evidence which prohibited a party from becoming a witness in his own cause. And yet the ablest legal minds of both the English and American Bar were long engaged in discussing this question before the experiment was finally made. Could that discussion have been conducted in the light of the experience now common to both countries under the actual operation of this new rule, it is more than probable that the old and cautious rule of the Common Law would never have been disturbed.

In this Country we are far removed from just complaint on this score, as compared with England, whose vast abuses, though largely relaxed and modified of late years, still hang heavy yokes around the necks of English suitors, and put no small amount of merited reproach upon the British Government; and this, too, notwithstanding the shafts of criticism and pungent satire have been long powerfully employed to produce a change. For years the Court of Chancery has been a by-word and a ridicule under the pens of some of the most accomplished scholars of England. Take, for instance, Southey's rasping sketch of "The Devil's Progress," in which his Satanic Majesty, while taking a circuit round the earth, is reported, among other observations, to have made the following:

"He heard a lawyer 'making the worse
Appear the better reason;'
And quoth he, 'friend Belial's seed hath grown
Much good fruit in its season.'"

And then, after the Devil has surveyed the world at large, you will remember, the poet recites that the cloven-footed traveler stepped down through the fogs into the Court of Chancery; and with the most woeful results both to himself, the profession, and the community at large. Thus runs his narrative, and thus he closes the volume that recites the Devil's journey:

"The Devil walked up Chancery Lane,
" And into the Chancery Court;
" Intending, like many who entered there,
" To make his visit short!
" But the *Printer's* devil—a little black imp!
" Is waiting for his *tail*; (tale)
" And swears—like a chip of the parent block—
" That his time and patience fail;
" So, all we can add to the present strain
" Is, *the Devil has not yet got out again!*"

And many of the people of England, to-day, believe with the poet that, sure enough, the Devil still maintains headquarters in that vicinity. But the aristocratic Lords and wise heads of the British Government, who, like the late Viscount Palmerston, manage somehow to maintain a respect for the manly art of pugilism, seem to think that even if this were so, they have the advantage of the Devil, after all, in this matter for they say, in the Saxon vernacular of the distinguished Tom Sayers, "Why, what fear need there be? have we not got him in Chancery?"

Now, all this, and a great deal more of the same character that might be cited from modern English literature, was designed for good, and doubtless has produced some wholesome changes, where so many are yet needed. But in this country, as already intimated, abuses are not so many, nor so hoary with age as "beyond seas." Consequently, the American lawyer, and especially the young lawyer, should be careful how he suffers himself to be led off on any wild crusade of legal reform. He should the rather, be careful and conservative in all he says, and does upon the subject. He should endeavor to uphold the Courts and all those well-tested rules and forms of procedure, constituting its code of practise, which, though possibly cumbersome in some particulars, do, nevertheless, furnish the very best mode of reaching truth in a sharp controversy over facts. Be cautious, therefore, and considerate; ready to sustain any rational change that may be approved by the Courts and the more experienced members of the Bar, but never suffering yourselves to be led blindly away into the chimeras, and quagmires, of that sort of law reform, which has pretenders for its framers, and demagogues for its advocates.

Without tarrying to press the obligations involved in the fifth clause of the oath, which affects more particularly your conduct and intercourse with professional brethren in and before the Courts, (and in reference to which the very best of words have been heretofore pronounced from this place by some of the ablest representatives of our profession, as well as by the accomplished head of this honorable institution). I pause but a moment on the sixth clause,—"not to encourage either the "commencement or the continuance of a suit from any motive of pas- "sion or interest."

Strange as it may seem, the wisdom of this rule of professional conduct does not, as a general thing, fully commend itself to the practitioner until after ten years or more of experience has demonstrated the weight of wisdom contained in it. The young Lawyer is apt to be altogether too eager for the parade of his first briefs, even to recall, much less carry out this injunction of his professional oath. In the causes of his early clients, he sees naught but justice and right; and is apt to exaggerate wrongs oftentimes existing more in fancy than in fact. He assures his already excited client that the Law as an armed champion, and ally, stands wait, ing for the coming battle with his opponent. He reads to him from his books some pertinent case to that under consideration, and the angry client forthwith draws the sword, and declares for war in this his very first interview with counsel. And oftentimes when this professional zeal is associated with an utter absence of moral principle, the client, reckless of results, is incited under color of law, to the very worst of deeds. Like Shylock, he cries—

"I stand here for law;
"I crave the law,
"The penalty and forfeit of my bond."

And so having the mere letter of the law in their favor, the lawyer and client together kindle and blow up the coals of strife and let loose, perchance, against helpless innocence herself, those demon passions of avarice and revenge, which, like coupled hounds, shall hunt her to her doom. In such hearts there is no pity, not even an instinctive sympathy with our common humanity. If appealed to for leniency or for some reasonable modification of a merciless demand, they do but reply, "Is it so nominated in the bond? I cannot find it; 'tis *not in* the bond."

Never thus suffer yourselves to kindle the angry passions of a heartless client, much less go forth with him in predatory chase of his helpless victims. On the contrary, rather make haste to quench the cruel flame by calm and judicious counsel, by imperative command, if necessary. Do not forget that as a minister and servant of that Justice whose birth is divine, you can never exile from your breast her attendant and favorite virtue, wherewith she mitigates the severities of her decree,—angelic and meek-eyed Mercy; and that

"The quality of mercy is not strained;
"It droppeth, as the gentle rain from heaven
"Upon the place beneath; it is twice blessed;
"It blesseth him that gives and him that takes.
"'Tis mightiest in the mightiest; it becomes
"The throned monarch better than his crown;
"His sceptre shows the force of temporal power,
"The attribute to awe and majesty,
"Wherein doth sit the dread and fear of kings.
"But mercy is above this sceptered sway;
"It is enthroned in the hearts of kings—
"It is an attribute of God himself;
"And earthly power doth then show likest God's,
"When Mercy seasons Justice. Therefore, Jew,
"Though justice be thy plea, consider this,
"That in the course of *justice*, none of us
"Should see salvation; we do pray for mercy.
"And that same prayer doth teach us all to render
"The deeds of mercy."

In direct connection with the commendation of this virtue, comes the last precept of the oath,—"not to reject for any considerations personal "to myself, the cause of the weak, the stranger, or the oppressed."

As long ago as when Columbus first turned the eye of Europe upon our Western World, the English Government passed a Statute to help the poor to their rights in courts of justice. It was entitled, "A "means to help and speed poor persons in their suits." By its means poor persons were to have writs, "nothing paying therefor," and the courts were obliged to assign to them, "counsel learned by their "*discretions*," (mark the language, for it expresses the highest form of professional wisdom) "which shall give them counsel, nothing taking "for the same; and all other officers necessary to be had for the speed "of said suits, which shall do their duties without any reward for their "counsel's help and business in the same."

But this rare old statute, beneficent as it was in its provisions, was, not a great many years back, held by Ch. J. Tindal to be but confirmatory of the rules of good mother Common Law, herself, who long bebefore this ancient statute, had conferred these privileges on the poor. (Brunt *vs.* Wardle, 3 Mann. & Grang., page 534.) In this country, as you are, doubtless, already aware, the same rule prevails; and the humblest and most wretched creature in the land, claiming its benefits, may, at any time command your services and mine to shield him from injustice and wrong, or secure for him a fair and impartial trial in the courts if arraigned as a culprit before the law. And these services, whenever claimed, you will, doubtless, render as cheerfully as the long line of your predecessors have ever done. But above all obligations of the law, either as statute or rule, if you regard the demands of this your oath, nay, more, if, as a man of integrity, you do but respond to the promptings of your own heart, "the cause of the "weak, the stranger, and the oppressed" will never make its appeal to you in vain.

The lawyer who recognizes his duties as a man of honor merely, irrespective of principle, will never suffer the truly friendless one to leave his office uncared for, or, at least, uncounselled. The retiring steps of the tearful widow, or of the trembling patriarch, turned without an audience from your door, will echo their complaints afar into that world where sits the Judge of the widow and the fatherless; and to these complaints, on the great day of Assizes, you will be called upon to answer. Nor will it do to dismiss this humble class of clients with the announcement, that the law, if such indeed be the case, affords them no relief. The resources of the Counselor's intelligence and experience, if seriously taxed, may devise some measure of help, some modified relief "*Sapiens dominabtiur astris.*"

There occurs here to memory a case illustrative of what may be done under such discouraglng circumstances, which I trust you will not think unworthy of the time occupied in its narration. In the summer of 1865, a lady, dressed in mourning, with a little child on either side of her and a babe in her arms, entered a Lawyer's office in this State, told her story and asked for counsel. That story was briefly this: Her husband, a Major in a Michigan regiment, had pressed his way down with the army of the Cumberland, and through all its battles, to the capture of Atlanta, when his term of enlistment expired, and he prepared to return home. But his regiment had neither Colonel nor Lieutenant Colonel, and the men were anxious that he should lead them with Sherman to the Atlantic, Although anxious to return again to his family and friends, he could not refuse their appeal. He therefore, volunteered his services for the great march, and led his regiment to the eastern coast. But while bearing a flag of truce, and a message from Gen. Sherman to Gen. Johnston, he received a traitor's ball, which ultimately resulted in death. The widow had applied to the Pension department, but was informed that inasmuch as her husband's name was not on the rolls of the Army when he was wounded, there could be no pension granted. She now interrogated her Lawyer whether she was indeed to be denied relief and left with her three children to perish from hunger and want? The Lawyer, after examination, was compelled to say there was no relief whatever under the laws. It was a sore announcement to make, but still more to receive. "Then God help me," she cried as she rose to depart, with her poor, helpless children clinging at her skirts. But before passing the outer door, she was recalled by the Counsellor. "There is no wrong," said he, "without its remedy, "and if we can't find one to-day we may to-morrow. You and your chil-"dren have given your all for the Country, and if existing laws do not "afford you relief, we must have some that will." Thereupon he took full memoranda of the facts stated, corresponded with various officers, from Gen. Sherman down to the Corporal who attended on the flag of truce, received from them all full corroborations of the sad story, and procured from State and Military authorities, ample testimonials as to the services and gallantry of the deceased. From these data he framed a memorial in the name of the widow and her children, addressed to Congress, and expressed in the most appropriate language his pen could command. With the memorial he sent a bill, providing that the name of the dead officer should be placed upon the roll of pensioners from the day of his death, and with the allotment appropriate to his rank. Senators and Representatives were next addressed upon the subject, and before three months had passed away, that bill had become a law, and a copy of the same, together with a check for the amount of money then due, embracing several hnndred dollars, were placed in the hands of the Soldier's widow. By this relief, that smitten and desolate family were rescued from absolute dependence and want, and engrafted into that great and sorrowing family of the Nation at large. The joy of the poor mother for herself and children, was altogether beyond her powers of expression. She insisted upon compensating her Counsel by an appropriation of the money received. He declined any fee at her hand, but his young son carries to Church every Sabbath, a beautiful English pocket-Bible bearing this inscription, "In grateful acknowledgement for professional services rendered by his Father to a Soldier's widow." Think you not that this Counsellor, who thus rose above the poverty of the law, and accomplished for his poor but worthy client, the relief she sought, appreciates this gift to his boy, far more than any pecuniary compensation that could have been bestowed upon himself? Ah! yes, there are fees and rewards in our profession, which, though not paid in dollars and cents, do yet and here, come back in blessings of peace, upon the heart of him, who rejected not " from any considerations "personal to himself, the cause of the weak, the stranger, or the op-"pressed."

The professional man, thus, fortified by his integrity, and faithful to his trust, will find all the better impulses of his nature acting in harmony with the obligations of his oath,—inspiring him to deeds of charity worthy of his high calling, and for the performance of which there flows a satisfaction wholly unknown to those who are strangers to such experiences. Such a man, too, can smile at the unworthy thrusts and flings of popular prejudice against the Law and Lawyers, which owe both their birth and continued existence to the abuses practised by bad men who have surreptitiously possessed themselves of the privileges and powers of the profession. Possessing the *mens conscia recti*, he can receive in silent indifference these taunts of his fellows even though backed (as they often are) by an ignorant attempt to turn upon the devoted heads of the profession, that stern denunciation of Scripture, "Woe unto you also, ye lawyers, for ye lade men with burdens "grievous to be borne, and ye yourselves touch not the burdens with "one of your fingers." This attempted imprecation loses all its force, when it is understood, that it is not the legal Counselors, but the religious teachers of the day that are here meant. And the perverted Scriptural admonition might be yet further answered, by recalling to the mind of the objector, the further fact, that about the only member of our profession spoken particularly of in the Bible, is Joseph of Arimathea, "a good man, and a just," who, as a Senator, and a member of the Jewish Sahnedrim that condemned our Lord, "*had not consented to* "*the counsel and deed of them.*" But who, in order to save the body of our Lord from the ignominious fate awarded the corpses of those executed criminally, wrapped it in linen, and laid it in his own new sepulchre, hewn out of stone, and located in his beautiful garden,—thus testifying, even more than his timid and scattered disciples, against the injustice of that midnight decree, founded on purchased and perjured testimony, by which human rights were overborne, and Innocence from Heaven itself, most wickedly condemned. It would be well, therefore, for some of our officious teachers and preachers too, to understand better their own Bibles, before they presume to pronounce in the name of their Master, their self-righteous anathemas upon that profession or body of men in whose charge are lodged all the rights and liberties of their fellow men.

And, now, without taxing your patience much longer, permit a concluding reference to that part of the Oath yet unconsidered, though found first in the catalogue of obligation,—"to be faithful to the Republic and Canton of Geneva,"—not, you will observe, to Geneva *first*, and *thereafter* to the Republic. The argument for true allegiance to the Republic *first* and *absolutely*, which lies directly upon the threshold of our National creed, need not here be explained. That discussion has passed. It was maintained in forum and battle-field, through four long and anxious years; but it closed with the last growling cannon of 1865. And God grant, for the peace of a land furrowed with its hundred thousand graves, that this question (which never ought to have been a question) may not again appear in either our political or military controversies. The true doctrine on this subject being accepted as settled, and in accordance with what were unquestionably the views of the Patriotic Fathers of the Country, the inquiry arises here, how otherwise shall the Attorney and Counselor prove himself faithful to the Republic? *First*, and most effectively, by actively putting his influence and service on the side, and ever in support of the Law.

In these reckless days upon which we seem to have fallen, there is, most unhappily for the future good of this Country, a manifest indifference to the enforcement of Law; and especially such laws as affect the good order and proprieties of life—shielding the Citizen in the safety of his person, and the enjoyment of his property. The grosser crimes of murder, robbery, and lust, have latterly multiplied so fast in the Land that the public mind appears to have become in a measure familiarized with them—nay, worse; in our larger cities "the rude fellows of the baser sort" seem actually to have robbed the honest citizens of more than half their corporate birth-right. For we see them in more than one great metropolis, strongly entrenched in their very Council Halls, whence they issue their robber-like edicts upon the treasury and resources of the people; and under the seal of the city successfully execute them. Indeed, public men, while they fall back upon the State authorities and the more virtuous Rural population, are to-day gravely discussing the question, whether the Republican form of government, so far as great Cities are concerned, is not, as a matter of fact, a failure. For under our theory of Government, which is not that of the one man's will—supported by a standing army—there is but a paper partition between us and Anarchy, and that is the Law—the Law in its purity and certainty of execution. Let the laws of the Country be but poisoned at their fountain-head, or their execution be committed to those who wilfully pervert, or divert their restraining influence, and it will not be long until, first our cities, then our larger and more densely populated communities, one after another (according to the spread of this popular demoralization) and finally, our entire people, shall be swallowed up in those sepulchral gulfs, where the once renowned nations of the Past have gone down to death, and a dreary oblivion.

Now, as the Lawyer, much more than the moralist, can appreciate the evils that must speedily ensue to the Republic from a general disregard of Law and all its just restraints; so the Lawyer, more than any other Citizen, can help to check and restrain the terrible mischief. Let him, whenever occasion calls for it, boldly take his stand in opposition to these men who thus affront the Law, and pollute her sanctuaries. His position once taken, good men of all classes will rally round him, and gladly give him their support. The latter want but a nucleus toward which to gravitate; and the Lawyer of sound morals and cultivated brains, soon becomes the animating spirit of the whole,—while they, who in the name of liberty, would license all those cancerous evils which strike not only at the peace but at the very security of social order, are driven back behind the pale of legal, if not of moral restraint.

And so, when any special and extraordinary excitement stirs the popular mind, like the School or Sunday law, or the Labor question, or any other topic springing out of the ever-changing character of our politics, over which the community has become roused, and riot and pillage threaten, like evil spirits, to break forth with flaming brand upon the city, then is it, that the high-minded and loyal Lawyer will cast himself into the breach, and by influence and eloquence, endeavor to stem the excitement;—to set up barriers against its wild advance, and guide it back within the permanent and peaceful channels of Law and Order. It is to him, before all others, that the masses of the Citizens look for defence in such hours of peril; for he knows the Law, and how quickest and best to avail himself of its securities to the public. They do not; and so all eyes are turned to him as a kind of civic, and if needs be, military leader in a combat with the mob. Oftentimes the highest form of physical and moral courage is required of him in emergencies such as these; but the true Lawyer neither hesitates nor flinches from his full duty. The clear, conscious knowledge he has of his rights, and the rights of those he essays to protect against a brutal and impassioned mob, as well as his experience in handling and controlling men by the power of the human voice, all embolden his heart, and make him confident of the Victory before the struggle fairly begins. Therefore it is, he is brave, often heroic, in upholding the Law and extending its shield over the head of the defenseless Citizen. And by such fearless discharge of duty is it, that the profession of the Law is commended to the public, In the hour when the hurricane and blaze of a riotous mob is raging through a City it is, that the people wake to a true appreciation of that profession, which, in the silken time of peace, is too often sneered at, and sometimes openly denounced as a moral nuisance in community--a cancerous sore on the body politic.

But woe, woe unto that lawyer, who, when the great bell rings its alarm for the Citizens to rally against the rising mob, shall be found lurking and herding with the riotous rabble,—retained in their interest by the promise of pay or political preferment,—mounting their rostrum, and under the specious words of liberty and right, inciting them on to deeds of violence and plunder. For such a Lawyer there is no justification—can really be no excuse. He knows full well that if any portion of community is oppressed with burdens too heavy for them, the Courts, or the Legislative Halls, are ever open for their relief, and thither is he bound to carry their complaints.

But when he makes himself one of these ruthless assailants of the Law, to whom he has formally dedicated his life and talents; and seeks to sanctify their wretched cause, by reflecting upon it whatever approval of the Law his poor position at the Bar enables him to impart, then does he not only openly violate his Oath as a Lawyer and a Citizen, but he is openly betraying Justice at her very altars, and striving to instal Anarchy in her room.

Of all and every such member of this honorable profession, now or hereafter appearing, it may be deservedly said, "the salt has lost its "savor—henceforth it is fit only to be cast out and trodden under foot of "men."

But the Lawyer, in taking in the full circle of duty, must look beyond his relations to the immediate community in which he dwells; he must also regard those wider and yet higher claims which his Country at large has upon his talents and services; and right cheerfully should he render them. For what to him is wealth or what is fame, what even all the sweet joys of family love, compared with that pleasure derived from a conscious assurance that, " all is well with the Republic,"—which, like a golden planet, high above the clouds that darken its lower sphere, sweeps steadily and ever brilliantly forward to glories yet unrevealed.

Would that we all might to-day enjoy the delights of such a pleasing hope! But it cannot be denied, that although the active presence of War is no longer before us, our Future is to-day clouded with doubt and apprehension. Before the late War, we had long and systematically ignored all those elements of sectional strife that strengthened with every year among us, and regarded naught but the thrift of corn and negroes;--hasting after Wealth, and that alone. We stubbornly refused to recognize the truth, that spiritual causes among a People work on in silence and secresy, revealing themselves at last in terrible and inexorable facts. And so it came to pass, that while we were busy pulling down our barns to build greater, there fell suddenly a voice from the silent sky above us, saying, "Thou fool! this night thy soul shall be required of thee, "and then whose shall those things be which thou hast provided?"

Whose, indeed? Let us not revive the agony of those four years in which the great majority of the people were held in dread suspense on this one thought! Shall they belong to the Nation so recently known the world round as the Uuited States? Or be partitioned off among several Nations, or several coalitions of Nations? Or fall a prey at last amid blood, and famine, and distress to the Foreign Spoiler? Then was it, that the American people first really waked to the great fact, that after all, the true glory of a Nation could not be built upon gold, or on cotton, corn, and negroes, that bring gold, but only on Truth, Knowledge, and Justice. We went down into the Valley of the shadow of Death to settle this great question of the National existence, and the God of Nations at last brought us through in triumph; but not until after we had wrought out this stern truth in our history also, which Providence has been so long teaching the Nations of the Earth.

But the tumult of this great strife is not yet abated, nor the cries of its distress hushed in the Land. Peace, if she is indeed unbound, and moves among us, comes wearing the red ribbon of danger in her yet disheveled locks. For the paths in which the Government is walking to-day, are slippery and perilous; and tangled and thorny is the thicket of public questions ahead.

Yet that portion of the American people who have struggled and sacrificed so much for the one grand and central Union of these States, have received their compensation. For they have developed latent powers, the existence of which was before unknown; their force of character has been revealed; their finest emotions have been touched and quickened; heroic statues and memorial piles of martyred brethren raised, with their eloquent lessons, on every hand; and the people have learned for themselves what true nobility lies slumbering in the great American heart. They know, too, that they have a great Nation still to preserve, with all its wealth of virtue and of valor; all its refined institutions for intellectual development and culture; all the splendor of success in the example they uplift to the people of other lands; and they know much better to-day how to preserve it than ever before.

So fully are they imbued with the spirit of free institutions, inwrought by this struggle with all the form and texture of their thoughts; so thoroughly, intelligently, and completely have they become possessed of the great principles of Freedom of speech, Freedom of press, Freedom of worship, security of person and property, and, above all, of the great American principle of Republican Government, that even if our common Constitution had been rent in that stormy strife upon the field, the liberty-loving portion of this People would again have met under some new Constitution adapted to their condition, in all the strength and power of consolidated Union. For they know that these great measures did not find their birth with the American Constitution, as once they were almost inclined to believe ; but had lived in the Earth long before, and that the Spirit of Liberty, which sprang from the bosom of the old Common Law, gave to us the chart of all these ; and in its appointed time gave us the Constitution also.

So that whatever may happen to us, even at the very worst, we must not fear; for back of our much-prized and venerated Constitution lies ever the broad field of Constitutional rights, with all the machinery of the Common Law, by which they are made available.

At no time, therefore, in the history of our Country, has there been such a call for learned and honorable Lawyers, as at the present. And they who are now entering upon this troubled stage, should come thoroughly furnished with all the learning of their profession, and especially with a thorough knowledge of Constitutional law ; the true rules of its construction, and its ready application.

Important changes are now necessitated in the Constitution of the United States; and Constitutional revisions are occurring in many of the States, North and West,—our own among the number—while new Constitutions entirely, have yet to be framed in the recovered States of the South. It is a time then, when mere "case Lawyers" must pass into comparative retirement, while those of the profession who know how to grapple with the gravest questions, and dispose of them promptly and successfully on principle, will pass directly to the front.

It is in such a time as this, young Gentlemen, that you are called to assume the duties and responsibilities of a profession, now very closely allied with the permanent peace and repose of the Nation. How cordially should you be congratulated that the long extended hours of toilsome study, are now giving way to those of active service! What powers of good to your Country, and your fellow men are now yours. How brightly breaks the day of promise before you; but still how inscrutable the record which each one has yet to make for himself. Under the high-toned instructions you have received from those who have here labored to enrich your minds with preparatory study, you have doubtless appreciated, and I hope endorsed, all that has been said in our examination of the Lawyer's oath. If this be indeed so, and you leave this Hall resolved to regulate your professional life by the principles we have found lodged therein, then may we safely predict for you a brilliant and successful career.

Take courage then, in this hour, which is apt to be one of despondency, if not of dread. And though you may think it long in the bud, be assured, if you are true Lawyers, the sweet flower of success will, in the time appointed, spring into bloom at your feet, and refresh your spirit with all its delightsome fragrance. Only accept, and rise to a full apreciation of the high calling and royal-like powers of your profession, and all will be well. Assume, in all the strength of your unsullied honor, its solemn engagements with God and your fellow men, " to do justice, " love mercy, and walk uprightly through life," and you will never have occasion to regret the choice you have made. " For he that walketh " uprightly walketh surely, but the perverse man, who walketh by " double paths, shall fall, and that right suddenly."

Remember, my young friends, (and it is my parting word with you at the threshold,) your escutcheon, to-day, is unstained,—and as yet uninscribed. Let your future and final years find it still bright, still and *ever* reflecting the highest virtues of your calling. So that when you shall have given place to those who follow after, they may find written thereon a noble record of manly virtues, professional honors, and National renoun. And to that end, may God speed you all!

www.ingramcontent.com/pod-product-compliance
Lightning Source LLC
LaVergne TN
LVHW011145110826
845150LV00008B/2520

* 9 7 8 1 4 1 8 1 9 2 3 8 9 *